Dichotomy of me:

a year of poetry on the madness and magic of motherhood

Ruth M Stacey

BookLeaf Publishing

India | USA | UK

Presentation by *BookLeaf Publishing*

Web: www.bookleafpub.com

E-mail: info@bookleafpub.com

ISBN:9789358317565

First edition 2024

DEDICATION

For my wonderful parents who guide me through the madness of motherhood and who always help me see the magic.

ACKNOWLEDGEMENT

Thank you to my beautiful son, Eddie, for making life so colourful. I hope you'll always know how much I adore you - I delight in you. I also hope, as you grow, you'll eventually know how hard I've tried - even in the darkest of times. Thanks, always, to my friends and family for their encouragement and the Instagram poetry and mental health communities that guide, support and navigate me through my new expression in poetry.

My husband, Pete (my sounding board) is always positive and complimentary of my writing and provides immense support for myself and Eddie. We are a lucky family.

PREFACE

My poems are all written in a very short time, straight into the notes on my phone and are pretty much unedited.

A 'stream of consciousness' style allows me to get taken in the moment - usually by an extreme emotion - and the physical act of writing provides a mindful catharsis that I'm hooked on!

If any of my poems provide insight, enjoyment or even guidance, somehow, then that is a pure bonus!

I connect with you

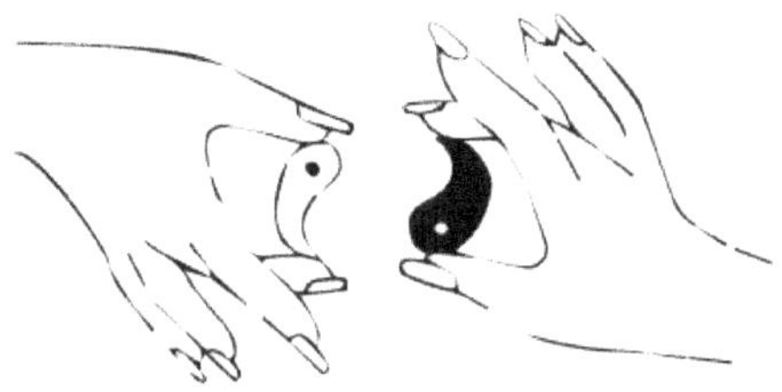

I connect with you
My button nose

Immeasurable bliss
Vulnerable hold

Simple kiss
Takes me back

Eyes closed in cot
Hair flat at back

Your skin so pale
And eyes closed tight

No need for milk
No strain for fight

Just soft pure bliss
Of sleep and calm

It takes me back
I start to yearn

But when I kiss
Your little face

You're not my three
But baby trace

You're mine to hold
As I am yours

Your dreams run wild
Through closing doors

You stare at me
And I face you

Kiss your nose
Connect with you

That

That I can make it better,
however it manifests.

That I can come to you,
call you, comfort you,
cocoon you,
coerce with you.

That we're a new 'us',
that I can't imagine myself
in a singular state anymore -
neither do I want to.

That you command me
to sing specific songs on repeat,
their essence serving to
soothe a needed familiarity.

Your fingers claw me,
mind implores me.

Questions repeating earnestly,
waiting my response and
every new word is savoured,
stolen, practiced, used,
repeated, learned, understood.

You contour my face with
probing fingers,
the hairs on my body gently
stroked,
yet a bite serves to investigate
upon a different day.

You cuddle and snuggle and
blow kisses and wave.
Your 'hiya' to welcome the day,
instantly bringing my first
welcome smile.

I delight in you,
hope to inspire your endless
interests and lend you safe love.

I'm your platform from which
to leap and explore,
to question and wonder and
worry and satisfy.

I'm a given,
I'm solid,
I'm yours.

And within all this, is the
total realisation that I never really
realised how loved I was,
until I had you.

A dull ache

Jaw-clenching,
Eye-shutting,
Lip-pursing,
Breath-drawing,
Fist-tightening,
Self-despairing,
Brow-furrowing,
Stomach-churning,
Regret-mongering,
Heart-quickening,
Eye-screwing,
Forehead-rubbing,
Sound-sighing,
Soul-sinking,
Dark-imploring,
Mind-melding,
Mistake-living,
Self-observing,
Critique-applying,
Black-dog thinking,
Self-reflecting,
Unaccepting,
Air-stifling,
Stomach-churning,
Out-of-body experiencing,

Mirror-gazing,
Head-shaking,
Non-accepting,
Wish-saying,
Prayer-repeating,
Wall-gazing,
Promise-rehearsing:
That I will be better.

I promise that I will be better,
Because you deserve it.

Is it weird when I'm ill?

Do the family calls dry up like a lake desperate
for water?
The dehydrated ground visible - vulnerable.

Or do the calls pile in,
muddled and rushing like
a river due to burst its banks?

Something must give eventually.
I have already 'given'.

Entering my weird world of an altered reality, a
fake truism, must disturb, perturb, frighten,
confuse.

The focus of our family pulled in - a black hole
of queries and questions:
Do we go along with her illness?
Do we challenge her new, temporary, fragile
belief system?

No, you just tell her that she's right and
everything will be alright:
Safe, safe, safe
Love, love, love.
Desperate eyes, a heart beating so erratically that
it doesn't know whether to feel excited or scared,
whether to run or challenge or
smile or laugh.

Doing all perhaps?
A simultaneous level of 'scare' to the
time-shattered onlookers.

No time for your own grief.
No time to shed your own harrowing tears.
Not now, although It. Will. Come
I promise.

Stick with me and my unpredictable
beast-of-an-illness.

Laugh when I'm crying and cuddle me like I was
your baby again because this world is ultimately
so new to me.

It scares me.
I don't know what to do!

I don't know how to feel and I keep getting it so
very wrong.

Put your lives on hold, onlookers -
dry your precious tears and lend me
your strength,
because I'll be back again.

I just need your presence and love and hugs and
reassurance to plug the terrible holes in my
altered mental reality.
My mental instability.
I'll love you back forever.

Is it weird when I'm ill?
Because, I'm so, so sorry.

Sea

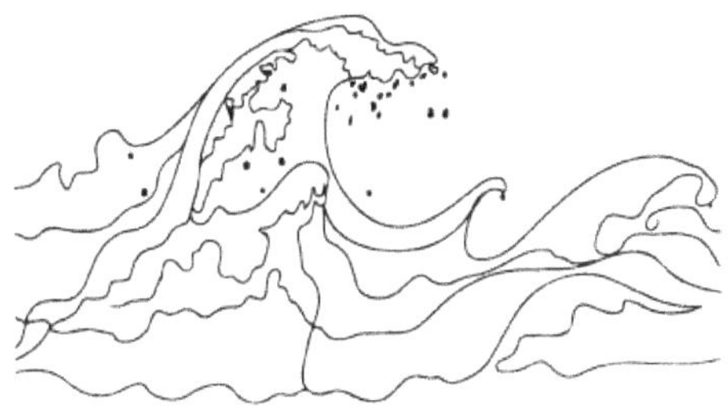

I breathe a deep sea breath,
fill my lungs with seaweed-tinged oxygen that
gives much-needed,
home-sense relief.

Beach-scanning,
treasure-hunting,
mottled rock pocketed,
secretly rolled between fingers.

Smooth sensation takes me back
to childhood beach days of
endless fun.
Time taker, time giver.

Endless skies: one becoming blue, another grey,
tinged with glasses-blurring spit.

The most mindful of days - mindless wondering,

gazing at temporary trampled footprints barely
left for enough time to etch a memory.

Then, an unexpected ripple of
white-wash-waves comes to make you jump,
laugh, smile, giggle, breathe.
Lung expansion.
Sweet, soul smiles - genuine, expansive.

Shells tinkle-crunch under light steps,
rocks crash-crunch,
giving way beneath -
falling up, falling down.

Seagulls cry their perfect-pitched cries -
'this is my home'.
I know. Mine too, really.

Mermaids' purses spied,
tangled seaweed spotted,
clicking shells collected -
each serves to savour a memory.

Splish-splat of your tiny feet,
you gazing at your own wibbly,
wet sea-trodden reflection.
An upside-down of you.

Mini feet trail mine -

our footprints of togetherness.

Seeing you running on a beach
just slows time to what
it really should be.

With minds and lungs clearing,
allowing capacious amounts of just sea-breeze
air to cleanse your soul.

We'll be back soon!
Wet hands, pebbled pockets,
calmed mind, smiled relief,
warmed hearts.

To slow our lives again from frenetic,
to wonderfully slow,
all played out in splashed reflections.

Mother Baby Unit (MBU)

Distant yet near,
Heart-wrenching,
Heart-healing,
Confused focus,
Hair-pulling thanks,
Deniable admission,
Crazed sanity,
Compelling kindness,
Suffocating slowness,
Halted healing,
Psychosis revealing,
Manic mothering,
'Too tight' cuddling,
Painted horizons,
Hypomanic revelations,
Doors closed,
Doors opened,
Small world widened,
Rosemary-scented serenity,
Glass-house-hospital,
Cared for, yet utterly alone,
Feisty independence,
Utter dependence,
Mouth fed (baby and me)
Medication denial,

Medication compliant,
Sleep saviour,
Sleep deprivation,
Clock-watching,
Corner-cowering,
Gritted teeth,
Forced smiles,
Form filling,
Mindfulness,
Food hater,
Food lover,
Baby carer - obsessor,
Never neglector,
Nightmares,
Daymares,
Dream giver,
Dream taker,
Minutes rush,
Days drag.

Where even am I?
Where are you all?

Reflection redemption,
Repeated affirmations:
I can, I Will, I am...

MBU: how can what seemed a nightmare
Have been my saviour?

I felt like the unluckiest person alive,
Our baby doomed but I face
A new reality of utter heartfelt appreciation,
Adoration.

How time changes and heals
And a warmth glows fondly in the hole that
Once was, a year on reflection of
My time in MBU.

I am

I am that woman in that hat.
That woman who you saw in the car window,
reflected confidently as you walked by.

The one who beams at her son's achievements,
laughs with him in loving togetherness.

The one whose cosy, soft grey morning
times are posted and shared - a mini window
into our beautiful, grey world.

I'm the mum who pops in and out of charity
shops in case a bargain rears its lovely head!
A game or a book or a toy for our son,
just to see his winning smile.
You've got me.

I'm the one who packs your lunch,

mindfully and carefully.
The one who takes such pleasure
in feeding you:
breast to bottle to fork!
Knowing I'm providing for you
and doing my best.

I arrange your clothes and sort your belongings,
breathe desperate intoxicating breaths,
keeping some clothes,
swapping others but a swell of pure
heart-warming happiness is always apparent
as I realise - I am your mum.
I hope I never take you for granted.

We go to baby groups,
I sing my heart out for you and
now you can accompany me with
the cutest of singing voices.

I am that proud, smiling mummy
who others smile at walking by.
My son may wave at you too!

I joined the 'mum club' after my
way-too-long wait but
sometimes, I just can't see it.

I'm too close to see,

too close to notice,
too close to breathe.
You don't stifle me - I stifle myself.

When I hear my 'other mummy' voice
shout and use harsh words,
I'll spend days with guilt eating away at me,
questioning my every mummy move.

Please help me to remember that
I am both these mummies,
but mainly the fun mummy he deserves.

Please let me pull myself up and remember,
not what I'm not but instead, what I am.

I'd live today again

I'd live today again,
I'd relish it
and I haven't been able to say that
for a while.

The pottering, mindful nature
of an autonomous day filled
with friends, family and love.

Conversations held not
frayed and regretted or forgotten.

A cloudless blue sky on which
to marvel at the hope of now
and the beauty of the future.

A smile reciprocated,
a hot coffee noticed,
hugs you meld into

not heart-breakingly tear
away from.

And simplicity appreciated -
like the longevity of safe sleep
and uninterrupted morning stretches.
Of being 'The Mummy Chair',
close enough to breathe in your
oaty hair as you play and explore
from your safe space.

That I am someone's safety,
made my heart sing.
Today.

Why not always?
We question our ability to see
the day-to-day truth.

So much muddle currently,
I can't see the flow,
let alone go with it.

But today, a friend bought me brunch,
listened and held me.

My husband smiled his smiley eyes at me and
my father held me strong.

These things made today count
and made me current,
visible, living.

Maybe they are there
every day for those who wish
to open their eyes and to live,
not just
exist.

Djembe Tot

You are my Djembe Tot.
My sky-reaching, life-screeching,
lit-eyed runner.

My music-inspired wonderer -
your gaze held high and
wild arms flow free.

A smile that ignites my heart
and lights the world:
your possibilities are endless.

The drums beat to your wonderful soul
or is it the other way round?

Room explorer, circle spinner -
no questions asked in this moment.
Just sheer joy.
Your boyish shrieks of 'it's great!'
fill the air around us.

I puff with pure 'mum pride',
adoring your eye-shut, eye-open concentration.
Mindfulness at its best in your two and
a half year old perfect bod.
The world lights you and, in turn,
you light the world.
I've never known pure pleasure like it -
to be in your company,
my little Djembe Tot.

This is life

I noticed the strawberries growing
just now as I walked down our lawn.
Today, I noticed the green richness of its colour
and was glad we turfed it,
gave it life, not critiqued its soily pockmarks.

My boy is tipping water, innocently,
down a slide and instead of rushing to
the adult guilt of wasted water (a lesson that can
wait),
I notice that he's looking at how chalk changes
when you apply it to wet cardboard than dry -
the colour intensifies.

And when the oven alarm beeps
and breaks my concentration,

I think of my son, healthily, heartily eating his
dinner and remind myself that
this is great and suddenly dinner doesn't seem a
chore.

Today.

Even pom poms cover the floor and sticky
fingers are grasping at things to applique, to
decorate a card 'to Daddy'. His idea.

And right now, I don't see the mess as
I move from my adjacent chair.
I see the tongue-poked-out concentration and
admire the empathy of our two and a half year
old boy, thinking of his Daddy's joyful face
when he receives his card.

He understands that this simple pleasure of
giving will be felt by both parties -
simultaneously, definitely
and will warrant a highly-prized 'Daddy hug'.

Today, the buzz-stuck-whir of a fallen
train strangely doesn't grate on my nerves.
Not when I look at you: lying down, parallel,
trying to understand the wheel-workings of the
world.

Pure fascination often happens in the midst of
disarray and I'm sorry that I sometimes miss it.

Thinking ahead or checking my phone or
gauging life by some absurd 'tidy barometer' that
my mind has created.

Today, I sat and was mindful:
I watched and listened and not only did I see you
smile more -
I felt mine.

Forlorn

Eye-lowered desperation,
Soft-blinked-shame,
Pricked tears threaten my face.

A quietness follows,
A needed quietness to stop the
Incessant judgment and noise.

So much noise,
Like a huddle of people in my mind jostling -
No turn-taking here,
Just pushing and shoving and screaming
Their ever-critical negative thoughts.

Who will win, I wonder?
Probably the one who shouts the loudest,
The one that looks up at life's secret
Camera (Imposter Syndrome in full swing),

And says 'I've cracked it!'
Cracked me, more like.

I can't fight anymore -
Haven't got the head space.
The thoughts don't flow.

I see an image of my worst self,
the worst yet to come and fear the worst -
That I am already who I never wanted to be:
The shouter,
The peace-breaker,
Threat-making,
Praise-retractor.

I see my scrunched face,
Angry,
Reflected in you
And hate myself.

Each time you defy me with a loud,
Desperate, deliberate 'SAKE' I know
That it is my face I see,
Reflected in you,
Not your beautiful, innocent self.
My ruination of life itself.

And I need to retract,
To run,

To isolate and reflect and judge away from
Lashing out and slamming doors and harsh
Words, from an uncontrolled whip-tongue.

You run rings around me
Until I have no more energy or patience or
Wisdom or will.
But still, you deserve more,
And I am currently of no use to anyone.

My day ended with you wanting to hit me
And started with that very action -
Right in the face.
Probably rightly deserved.
My love - you deserve more than me.

I stood tall today

I stood tall today and noticed the top half of the world: the roof tops merging with blue sky, not the tips of toes treading dark pavements.

My eyes creased with the sight of the sun that warmed my smile and the breeze whipped the wispy hair around my face.

I was aware of so much brightness,
taking in the world as it is rather than dark
versions of events that haven't happened - might
never happen.

It's funny how a 'head up' day means awareness
of the tops of everything,
like looking up is so much more than simply,
looking UP!

It's the 'taking in' and the noticing and accepting
of 'what is' not what 'might be' in this real-world
version, that really matters...

The clouds move past the sky and things change
and move and manifest.
They aren't stuck.
I'm aware, funnily, of the top half of my face
like my eyes are in charge of my smile now, they
negate my furrowed brow and my nose pricks
with summer scents.
Gone are the pursed lips of the one that doesn't
want to join the world.

I joined it today. It was a Head Up day today, an
'I belong' day, an 'I put make up on' day, a
ponytail swishing (washed hair) day and a day to
notice all the light that today I cannot ignore.

The summer-blue sky is simply a nicer view to
take in than the blackened concrete I tred - it has
so many more possibilities.

I honour to try my best, daily, to simply look up
and stand just that little bit taller, for the view is
just so much brighter.

Spring's noisy silence

The soft air whispers joy across my face –
its light coolness welcome as
the spring sunshine finally emerges.

Birds' shrill sounds of song spread wildly
through the greenery,
a conversation of positivity across their
sun-soaked home.

The world surely seems still and
my poorly, pockmarked boy
rests gently,
his closed-sleeping-baby eyes
allowing a welcome break to his temporary,
wretched state.

And the sounds that surround me now are gentle
and not pressing:
a passing train tick-tacks along tracks and

I almost exclaim, "a train!" to my absent son
but just now his ears will ignore my rushed
words.

Washing flit-flutters in the breeze and
still-beige leaves tinkle against their branches –
the last 'holders-on'.
They will need to give up their wintry hold soon,
submit to spring and summer, finally.

I raise my face to the sun - cat-like,
a seated Sun Salutation,
embracing, enjoying the red zig-zag pattern
on the backs of eyelids,
a strange, warm blind-sight.

A new playhouse sits still, waiting,
Bleeding Hearts break open their pink-red
beauty and Peonies pierce with hope.

Planes drone across the sky with
secret destinations and promises.
A distant drill symbolises a neighbour's
home-improvement-hope,
a catching vibe that I'm sure will spread
and echo as warm days pass and lengthen.

The garden has a silent, synergy of soft joy.
Even books sit next to me closed,

urging me to open them and dive into their
wonderful, playful pages –
a whole new other world to enjoy and watch
play out inside my now quietened mind.

My shoulders sink into themselves slowly
and a chair provides welcome support.
I feel my whole being melt-relax into the
sunshine, drinking it up, absorbing its healing
properties.

Utterly taking in this precious moment of
mindful stillness,
allowed only by tuning into the nowness of
spring's noisy silence.

I adore your presence

I adore your presence, your body,
I doubt I even know my own as well.

I can picture you top to toe -
the desire to memorise your whole being
is overwhelming at times.

Tonight, you hung on to me and
pleaded for me to stay with you
until you fell asleep.

I saw your dark, sweaty hair falling
on your perfect, pale face -
a curl that falls forward gently upon it.
Lighter at the front, tumbling down barrels at the
back that curl vertically.

And the fluffy fuzz at the back where you sleep
that I know you'll complain about when I
untangle in the bath -
all are your beautiful 'curly woos'.

One day, you cried in the bath when I tipped
water over your hair,
but not because the water upset you,
but because you caught your reflection
in the metal of the bath and said you were sad
because your curls had gone!

'I want them back Mummy!'
They delight me and others and you've learned
to say 'thank you' when someone compliments
your red hair.

When your eyes are closed,
I truly wonder at the length of those lashes that
sometimes are a little lost behind your new
glasses.
That yawn - the elongated 'O' - instantly takes
me back to baby you.

Your pouty, full lips (with that year-old white
split-lip-scar) and that wonderful profile: the
flatness on the top of your nose, the slight flick

of the button bit that I recall so utterly clearly at
our five-month scan.

Your high hairline and soft, soft brows
really define your face now and your eyes
sparkle especially now with your wicked sense
of humour - you are so much fun.

Your neck is delicious - even the dry patches of
your skin that I need to tend to carefully and
your sore eczema - it's all so you.
So loved.

Your rough little fingers, I'd know anywhere,
I love.
I'm always surprised by the softness of other
little one's hands but none are yours but those
I know, that cling to me tonight more so.

Your tiny birthmark on the back of your right
arm was located the other day when you
marvelled at mine on my foot attentively
applying cream to where you think I needed it
and 'to soothe your sore feet mummy'.

The strawberry on your tummy is just a faint
memory now,

almost completely gone and now a sweet,
prominent mole graces your perfectly pale
tummy.
Always our little pot belly but also so strong and
lean and athletic for a little bod.
You're growing so finely.

You'll happily let me cut your fingernails -
our manicure sessions,
but oddly, never your toes so your nails
curl over until they are dirty and broken,
but still they are yours. And mine.

And now, I've noticed recently the downy
growing-up hairs on your legs which pitch you
as a little boy and I hear you clearly state, 'I'm
not a baby, I'm a boy' and I remember -
no-one told me I'd love my boy more than my
baby!

Your breath, hot and sweet, deepens and your
grip lessons as I breathe in a complete
appreciation that you are here with us
and I let go, just for the night.

I'll be here in the morning, my beautiful,
beautiful boy.

I brushed your hair

Today, I brushed your hair too roughly
trying to rid it of its frequent matting at the back
(even though the touch of it makes me think of
just you).
And, I didn't listen to your cries of refusal or
release you in your struggle to get free.

I was in a silly mummy-meld aiming for an end
goal of 'brushed hair' for nursery,
put off for too long because you had become
unwell.

I battled with you when you refused your dinner
and argued childishly over whether you would
eat first and then get TV,
or in your mind have TV first and then you'd eat,
but I didn't want to lose that fight either.

So, your dinner ended up in the bin and although
I offered you rice pudding,
you were cross at me so ate none.
I said you could be frustrated and dislike me,
in that moment.

But then came the medicine arsenal:
Piriton for your itchy skin, a plethora of creams,
Calpol to get your temperature down and cough
medicine to halt your hacking cough, day 12,
and inhalers to ease your wheeze and by then,
I think we have both lost the plot!

There is love in these actions and panic-driven
parenting but it's followed by self-hatred and
dread: I am the mum I don't want to be,
AGAIN.

But when your tiny voice comes "I'm sorry for
saying 'yuck' to dinner and for not letting you
brush my hair",
my apology is already prepped from sodden eyes
- an attempt to let you know that it all comes
from love even though it doesn't feel like it.

These jobs are often 'mummy jobs',
getting through the things that I know are not
'your favourite' -

they can be done with a calmer hand and softer
touch and I don't know why I didn't use that.
What fuels this temporary mummy madness?

A promise again to myself that I won't focus on
the goal and lose who you are in the process,
even if you have gone to bed happy, soothed,
cared for, comfortable.

What once was a cute 'Daddy' cry,
now pains me with utter rejection -
I can't soothe you most of the time when
weekends come.

We are each other's world for two days
of the week, we are one: my love, my life, my
boy.

Yet, as the week ends and weekend nears,
I know I'm entering the part of my week that I
find the hardest
due to the sheer level of rejection I face.

And no matter how much I know that you don't
mean it,
that you push away the parent you're closest to,
I feel the pain so rawly and feel damned.

The true rollercoaster of my mummy emotions:
the highs, the lows,
my reality.

To go fly a kite

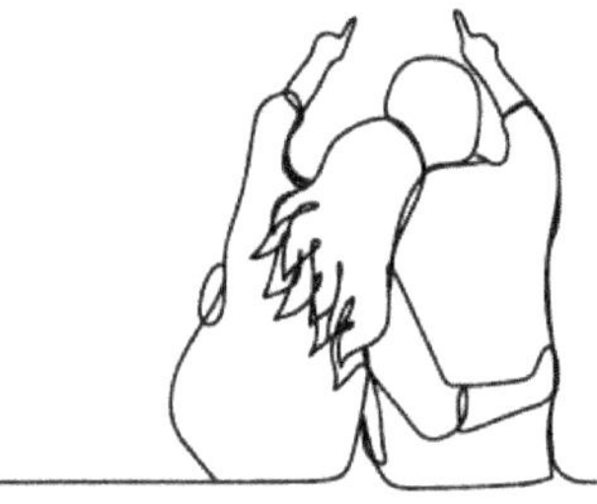

How deliciously mindful to go fly a kite!
Something, perhaps, I haven't done since I
Was a kid.

To stare up into blue-white skies,
Clouds billowing, swish-swirling,
Ends meet beginnings.

To laugh a shriek-laugh,
Not prepared or harboured or stored,
Just plentiful in its spontaneity.

To smile a smile so cold and wild
That your teeth dry!
The centre of my back - a freezing cold,
The centre of my heart - the complete
Opposite.

To hear tiny words of 'my face is SO cold'

But to hang-cling on to the moment
Because you know that memories
Are being made in these cold 'firsts'.

The ones you sometimes feel are forced,
Then realise it's because you are reaching
Into your childhood past for a memory that,
Although buried deep, stirs simple joy and
Similar wide-cold smiles.

And the shrieks you now hear are yours and
Your son's.
A wrapped-up-warmth, running along
With a sky-bound butterfly.
Freedom personified.

To breathe that deep, life-fulfilling air,
And know that at times like this -
Life seems to stop still.

To stare up into blue-white skies,
To see a butterfly flittering its many colours
And my son's lit up face as we together
Run.

The dichotomy of me

I have bipolar but bipolar doesn't 'have' me,
usually.
Usually, I self-care but haven't recently.

Started to self-hate,
a thing I never thought I'd start this late in life.
Feelings of pure despair and self-loathing.

A desperation to just escape, run, leave.
But sometimes when I wonder the
'What if I didn't?'

A slammed door is bad enough,
the negativity and dullness of my uncoping
world ricochet through our house,

my white-blind-mind chooses not to picture the
exact expression on my son's face when I left.

Did he cover his ears? Flinch? Cry?
Huddle in a corner?

The other day we cried together
(my tears are easier than my anxiety-anger, to
bear, I truly know that).

He said he didn't want me to shout,
I said I wanted him to let me put him to bed and
not cling on and obsess with daddy or disturb
him when he sleeps.
My son asked me to lie with him, moments after
I shouted right at him.

It puzzled me how he wanted me then,
but I suppose he knew he could have me calm
and close and nuzzling next to him to sing him
'Baa, baa' until his breathing reached that steady
slow of sleep.

When I breathe my biggest smile-breath of the
day, feeling I've done something right.
Unconditional love seems to go both ways.

Days can go on and on and on and on

and I wouldn't want anyone else to mother my
son.
I know how to get it right but sometimes I just
cannot access it...

Sometimes, the repetition of motherhood is
madness personified.
When the only thing I hear in a whine is a pitch I
simply cannot abide and an 100th time cry of 'I
need cream' or 'Daddy' that compassion should
greet,
are just words: the source of a relentless,
Chinese water-torture-type-affair.

Just the repetition that makes me temporarily
insane, sometimes.

And the bipolar me - who I keep at bay most of
the time - is exacerbated by the dichotomy of
motherhood.

I'm proud of myself

I'm proud of myself today
I think
The pulling dredging desire to stay put
Under covers turned into a 5km run
And the current shower-dodger in me
That raises its head when I'm low
Allowed my body to be graced by warm
Flowing water
And I did enjoy it

And I read today
I may have had to read each page more
Than once to gather the
Meaning of someone else's life
But I revelled in the escapism

And when I desired a drink and felt the
Familiar pull of the great sofa slump

I got up and made myself something to eat
To nourish myself

And I smiled albeit definitively forced
I did it
And when my husband and boy came home
Into my quiet peace I'd tried to hold so
Tightly onto
I think I smiled back and listened to the
Rambling excitements of my little one's day

And really I'd rather have had my head
Stuck in a book
In someone else's life but somewhere
I found the courage for cupcake making
Although I was short and sharp in
My instructions and lacking in praise
I still did it

And on realisation that there was no
Obvious dinner for me to now prepare for
Myself and husband
I didn't fall into the heap I'd thought
Against the refrigerator door
I breathed deeply and poured myself a
Glass of wine and whipped up a dinner to
Be proud of

Yes I raised my voice today

And yes I shut myself away for 20 minutes
To delve into my alternative book world
Where I live but am not in charge
With no responsibilities and where life flows
From page to page

But when upstairs upon hearing my
Husband 'battle' with my child
I didn't sink deeper into my bed or
Shut my ears from the offense
I went down calmly and located engaging
Activities that might slow and stop his
Current misplaced fists and it did

I helped him count and read
Tracing his tiny finger around figures or
Letters
The teacher in me beaming

And upon bedtime I ensured that he knew
How happy and proud I was of him and
What he'd accomplished in the day
Only to realise that upon waking
This morning my only desire was to stay
And be warm in my bed

So tonight I'm not only going to reflect on
My son's accomplishments but my own

In times of sadness, hardship, sorrow and
Uncertainty
I am
Trying my best

I may never

I may never
See those two pink, tiny
Meaningful lines again
And feel that overwhelming rush
Of who to call, to contact
To hear those congratulations

But I do feel highs
In other everyday things
When my boy, today, added
A steering wheel, lights, luggage
And stairs to his bus drawing
'In case it breaks down mummy'

And in those wonderful things
They say that stop you in your
Tracks: "I'm tired, Eddie," I said
Today whilst pushing him and his trike
Uphill and his reply: "Don't worry,
Mummy - you can have a nice lie
Next to me when we get in
And I'll keep you safe"!

That same desire to share the
Momentary pride, although different in

Nature
I may never see my belly swell
Again, to bond in that same sense
With something incredible going
On inside me but I will and can
Become strong in my body once
Again with my son beside me:
Yoga, stretching, running, dancing
And actually feel relieved at my
Body seeming to finally return to
Pre-baby boobs and tum

I may never reach out to my
Unsettled infant in their 'Next to Me' crib
Knowing that just
My patting hand or Shattered-shhhhhing
Will send them to sleep but I do know
Where to place the weight of my
Arm on my three years old's body
At bedtime and how to rendition
'Baa, baa' at an ever-slowing and
Silenced pace to lull him to sleep

I may never have those gorgeous
Baby mornings, you squidged
Cosily into your 'Snuzpod' on your
Back between my husband and me
With nothing to do of a morning
But stare in awe and wonder

But now...at 3 and a 1/4, I get to
Actually read a book next to you
Whilst you're happily lost in 'Spidey and His
Amazing Friends' - my odd sideways
Glance entranced by your
Sideways smile, munching obsessively on
Cheerios with milk
Finally feeling these 'little wins'
They said would come with time

So my body certainly would like to
Go back and do it all over again
And my heart absolutely knows
How to love so strongly again and
Again
I'm sure

But, I have to know my limits and I
Don't play the 'I have mental health conditions'
Card very much -
Ever really - but I certainly feel
After the evil that was Postpartum
Psychosis and the struggles that
Face me daily that I
Metaphorically have
'KNOW YOUR LIMITS'
Tattooed on my head

And now that I'm surrounded by mothers with

Their second babies, my feelings
And emotions tug, this way and
That - I feel the weight of it
Endlessly these days

But it's not that I've made the
Wrong decision to stick to one
It's that there never really seemed
To be the choice
For me, anyway

So for now, I'm super-happy for my
Friends
Super-sad, deep down but feel I
Can manage both emotions at the
Same time

Because I feel I'm doing
Something right: you can write
Your name, draw detailed
Awesome pictures, dance and sing
Like a popstar-rockstar, have incredible
Empathy and a hilarious sense of humour
Already, can share well,
Are kind...oh, and, you let me read
My book in the mornings whilst
You're busily, happily, indulgently
Munching
On Cheerios and milk

I don't crack a smile

I hate the days when
I don't crack a smile,
where parenting itself
seems such a trial.

The minutes drag on
and moments meld,
my child tries to connect -
tries to be held.

But I'm stuck in the motion
of doing the action,
but lacking in applying
my usual compassion.

And a part of me wants
to break out and be free,
to spend the whole day
just feeling me.

This downward gaze
just misses so much,
and oddly, I do crave
a wish to be touched.

By total paradox,
I wish to be left alone,
so as not to mess with the
safety of home.

"Mummy, where are you?"
I just need a rest,
head in my hands,
no ability to jest.

To cajole or to sing
or make things better,
my normal self,
such a go-getter.

Quite capable, really,
of turning things around,
the smile has now gone -
replaced with a frown.

I desperately look for
advice online -
for parenting tips
that I wish could be mine.

But application seems
impossible today,
I'm 'back brain' functioning,
I don't want to play.
And guilt rushes in as I hear
"Are you happy?"
from my four year old's voice,
he's still just so chatty.

He calms and regulates
which I must also do,
but my mind currently
does not have a clue.

And I'll lift, I know,
out of this bad state,
to turn it around and
to reinstate:

my jovial, nature,
positive parenting,
the mummy that laughs
and will often sing.

But today I'm not me and
I don't want to be mummy,
don't want to laugh or
try to be funny.

So we're trapped in a state
of pure aggravation,
and in my son's voice,
I hear my intonation.
So, I have to try and
slope off this dark mood,
to strive to be nice and
not to be rude.

Because I'm a mum,
more than I'm me,
and the joys of this role,
usually plain to see.

An off day, just that,
not the end of the world -
tomorrow's another day,
I know I am told.

In your absence

In your absence
My wandering mind
Is drawn to you
To anchor my love
In your pure physicality

Like the words alone
In their simplistic nature
Can conjure up the 'you'
In you:

Your perfect form
Your tiny bod
Your fluted, reddened lips
The soft 'V' of downy hairs
That glide secretly down your back

Silky-red barrel curls that I
Mindfully caress between my

Fingers
The scent I inhale from the back of
Your baby-soft-skin neck

Pale, even skin - matt and almost
Powdered dimples with a
Certain cheeky smile
That often plays upon your young face

Fine, though thickening, brows
Frame those brown eyes that
Never cease to wonder
Your button nose (please always be a button) -
I'll kiss with delight

All to ignite the You
I cannot right now see
But still the physicality of love
Appears to me